THE UNITED STATES
CONSTITUTION

I0558795

EDITIO PRINCEPS LATINE

David Kovacs, PhD., translator

John Kevin Newman, PhD., editorial reviewer

The background for this translation was first presented to

The Chicago Literary Club

by

Harry L. Stern

March 4, 1996

Cover design by Harry L. Stern III

Front cover: Cicero. Marble statue in front of the Old Palace of Justice in Rome. Licensed from Dreamstime.com.

Back cover: Preamble and Article I of the U.S. Constitution. Public domain, obtained from Wikimedia Commons.

Published by Quill Hawk Publishing

Printed in the United States of America
Available from Amazon.com and other retail outlets

ISBN 979-8-9869102-8-4 Paperback

To the memory of Harry L. Stern, 1930-2020

Contents

Foreword

My father, Harry L. Stern, originated the idea of translating the U.S. Constitution into Latin in 1977. After nine years of struggling with it himself, he finally enlisted the services of the finest modern writer of classical Latin prose, Professor David Kovacs of the University of Virginia, who produced a complete translation. In 1988, in anticipation that the translation would soon be published, my father wrote the Preface and Professor Kovacs wrote the Translator's Preface. Alas, more years went by without publication. In the 1990s, my father wrote the background material about Cicero (Part I), the five Founding Fathers who comprised the *Committee of Style* (Part II), and his own study of Latin (Part III), which he presented to the Chicago Literary Club as an essay titled *Peregrinantur, Rusticantur* in 1996. Although my father continued working in his profession as a rare book dealer and appraiser right up until his death in 2020 at the age of 90, he never published the translation. I resolved to see the project through to completion as a lasting tribute to his memory. A few details of his life follow.

Harry L. Stern's lifelong interest in travel and languages was sparked by a trip to Europe with his mother in 1947. He graduated from the Latin School of Chicago in 1948 and Yale University in 1952, where he majored in Classics. Following his service in the U.S. Army (1952-1954), in which he was posted to the National Archives in Washington, D.C. to translate captured German and Russian documents, he continued his study of languages at the University of Geneva (1954-1955). Afterward, he remained in Europe and sold books in France and Germany. He settled in Chicago in 1957, where he worked in the family grocery business. In 1965, his interest in antiquities and historical documents led to a job with Kenneth Nebenzahl, a world-renowned dealer in antiquarian books and maps. In 1975, my father started his own business in the same field, turning his classical training and love of languages into a long and enjoyable career. He also earned a Master's degree in American History from the University of Chicago in 1991. He was a long-time member of the Antiquarian Booksellers' Association of America, the Chicago Map Society, the Chicago Literary Club, the Caxton Club, and the Grolier Club. He was beloved by his family and colleagues alike.

Latin is literally embedded in our institutions and currency. Above the east and west doors of the U.S. Senate Chamber are inscribed *Annuit Coeptis* (God Favors Our Undertakings) and *Novus Ordo Seclorum* (A New Order of the Ages),[1] the same phrases that appear on the one-dollar bill above and below the pyramid, on whose base is written MDCCLXXVI – the year 1776 in Roman numerals. Over the presiding officer's desk in the Senate is the motto *E Pluribus Unum* (Out of Many, One), which is embossed on all U.S. coins. But the connection between Latin and our government goes well beyond mottos.

"The roots of the Constitution are in classical antiquity." So begins the article by Bonventre[2] that traces the influence of classical thought on our form of government. Not only were the Framers of the Constitution well acquainted with the classics through their early education, they also prepared themselves for the Constitutional Convention of 1787 by reviewing ancient history and political thought.[2] According to Bonventre, "Cicero recommended a commonwealth containing a 'royal element,' some 'influence of the aristocracy,' and 'certain matters reserved to the people.'" The Framers implemented this recommendation in the form of a President, a Senate, and a House of Representatives. This mixed form of government was meant to strike a balance that would prevent one element from dominating the others and descending into either tyranny, oligarchy, or mob rule. There is much scholarship on this topic, such as the books by Richard[3] and Ricks,[4] to name but two. The common lessons are (1) the Framers' deep understanding and appreciation of the classics shaped not only their ideas of how to form a government but also their moral character regarding the importance of virtue and the placement of the common good above factional interests; and (2) the classics are still relevant today, with much to teach us in our own fractured times. The present volume extends the notion of classical influence on the U.S. Constitution to its ultimate conclusion—a translation of that document into a classical language.

I hope that this volume becomes a standard text for students and scholars of Classics, Constitutional Law, and American History, and a collector's item for bibliophiles, as my father would have wished.

Harry L. Stern III
Seattle, August 2023

[1]https://www.senate.gov/about/historic-buildings-spaces/chamber/overview.htm

[2]Bonventre, Vincent Martin. A Classical Constitution: Ancient Roots of our National Charter. *New York State Bar Journal*, December 1987.

[3]Richard, Carl J. The Founders and the Classics: Greece, Rome, and the American Enlightenment. *Harvard University Press*, 308 pages, 1995.

[4]Ricks, Thomas E. First Principles: What America's Founders Learned from the Greeks and Romans and How That Shaped Our Country. *HarperCollins Publishers*, 416 pages, 2020.

Prefatio

Profiteri libet cuius rei gratia hoc opus edendum curarim. Multos iam annos bibliopola sum, et inter eos numerandus qui libros remotioris aetatis emunt et studiosis rerum antiquarum rursus vendunt. Quod negotium ut commoda multa et iucunda affert, ita nullum iucundius quam quod inter scripta maximi momenti maximeque memorabilia eorumque auctores cotidie versor.

Plus viginti annos praecipue cordi curaeque sunt libri qui paulo ante libertatem Americanam fundatam pauloque post editi sunt, quorum ex numero satis saepe mihi in manibus erant Constitutionis, quam dicunt, Americanae antiquissimae editiones, necnon alia opera quae cum hoc documento coniuncta sunt.

Quam Constitutionem qui princeps eorum fuit qui litteris mandarunt, Jacobus Madison, classica, quam dicunt, eruditione penitus imbutus erat, linguasque antiquas, sicut plurimi ex aequalibus eius, optime callebat. Nec mirum: quo enim tempore litteris in Universitate Princetoniana operam dabat, mos erat studia perficientibus opus quoddam Latine scribere et idem Latine viva voce defendere.

Multis abhinc annis mihi in mentem venit Constitutionem nostram haud aliter scriptam esse quam si ex Latina versa esset. Quam rem minus mireris si tecum reputes quota pars studiorum in Universitatibus eorum temporum ex litteris antiquis constiterit. Inde fit ut opus haud dissonum ab institutis et doctrina patrum nostrorum prolaturus sit si quis Constitutionem Latine vertat. Quod opus nunc perfectum speramus fore ut novum quoddam lumen Constitutioni addat necnon litteris antiquis.

Preface

I would like to say a few words about my reasons for undertaking this project. I have been an antiquarian bookseller for some time. One of the delightful aspects of this business is the daily contact with some of the great works of historical significance and with their authors.

The era of the American Revolutionary War and the early years of the American Republic has been my specialty for more than twenty years. Several of the earliest printings of the United States Constitution have passed through my hands, as well as a number of the ancillary works associated with this foundational document.

James Madison, the principal author of the Constitution, had an education deeply rooted in Classical learning, and he knew the Latin and Greek languages well, as did many of his contemporaries. At the time he was a student at Princeton, most theses were composed, and oral examinations conducted, in Latin.

It occurred to me many years ago that the Constitution often reads like a translation from Latin. This is not so surprising when one considers how much of the college curriculum in that period was Classical. Consequently, a Latin version of the Constitution seems to be a natural extension of the education and thinking prevalent in the era of the Founding Fathers. We hope that it will add a new dimension to the study of our Constitution and to the field of Classical Philology.

Ut de me ipso pauca referam, profiteor me lingua Latina legenda, scribenda, explicanda, quae studia gaudeo me xii annos natum incohasse, etiam nunc delectari. Qua pro delectatione gratia habenda est patri avoque meis, qui et ipsi his litteris in universitate operam dederant, et quorum libris in meis studiis utebar, necnon magistris multis linguae Latinae quorum amor erga antiquos in me haec studia fovebat, imprimis magistro in Schola Woodbury Forest Virginiensi Harry Bowman et Professori in Universitate Yalensi Clarence Mendel, demortuis ambobus.

Harry L. Stern
Dabam Chicagine mense Ianuario anno p.C.n. 1988.
[Translation by David Kovacs]

On a personal note, let me add that the study of Latin composition grammar, and literature, which I was fortunate to begin in junior high school, has remained an enduring interest throughout the years. For this lifelong enjoyment, I must thank my father and grandfather, both also Latin majors in college, whose books I continued to use during my own academic career; and, of course, the numerous teachers of Latin whose inspiration and enthusiasm helped nurture this interest, most notably the late Harry Bowman of the Woodbury Forest School in Virginia, and the late Clarence Mendel of Yale University.

Harry L. Stern
Chicago, January 1988

Praefatio Interpretis

Cum a me abhinc plus duobus annis petiisset bibliopola doctus Chicaginiensis Harry L. Stern ut Constitutionem, quam dicunt, Americanam Latine eo proposito verterem, ut annum ducentesimum rei publicae nostrae insigniore quodam honore afficeremus, magnopere gavisus sum. Quamquam enim non nesciebam quantum laboris susciperem, ut qui locutiones Latinas et rebus et verbis modernis idoneas excogitare conaturus essem, iucundum tamen et operae pretium putavi eorum sapientiae et prudentiae aliquot hebdomades incumbere qui huius rei publicae fundamenta iecerunt. Quod tempus ut solutus omni negotio operi impendere possem, liberalitas permisit patroni [Harry L. Stern], nec non ut versionem perlegeret castigaretque vir doctus J.K. Newman, in Universitate Illinoiensi litterarum antiquarum professor, cuius monitis haud pauca debere versionem meam libenter profiteor.

Ea est linguae Latinae natura ut nonnumquam quae in eam vertuntur lucidiora clarioraque fiant. Haud raro enim accidit ut ambigua quaeque, si in linguam Ciceronianam vertenda sunt, omissis ambiguitatibus vel consulto factis unum solum sensum exprimere cogantur, et quae locutiones vagae et a sensibus nostris et rebus abstractae sunt, quibus locutionibus abundant linguae hodiernae, eae omnes ad res redigantur et concretam quandam sententiam habeant. Quapropter usui fore hanc versionem iis spero qui de Constitutionis significatione disputant, nam sensum quem minime quaesitum (quamvis non semper maxime in promptu) esse arbitrabar semper reddidi.

Translator's Preface

When the learned Chicago bookseller Harry L. Stern asked me more than two years ago to translate the U. S. Constitution into Latin to celebrate in a special fashion the two hundredth anniversary of our commonwealth, I was delighted. For although I was not under any illusion about the difficulty of the task of rendering its modern words and ideas into suitable Latin, I thought it would be pleasant and worthwhile to spend time in careful study of the wisdom and sagacity of our Founding Fathers. The means to devote myself to this task free from the distraction of other work were supplied by the generosity of the publisher [Harry L. Stern], who also arranged for J.K. Newman, Professor of Classics at the University of Illinois, to read and criticize a draft. I am happy to acknowledge that my version owes a great deal to his suggestions.

It is characteristic of the Latin language that translation into it frequently renders the subject-matter clearer than before. Ambiguous expressions commonly must lose their ambiguity (even intentional ambiguity) and express a single meaning in order to be rendered into Ciceronian prose, while vague and abstract expressions, so plentiful in all the modern languages, must be rendered particular and concrete. It is my hope, accordingly, that this translation will be useful to interpreters of the Constitution since it attempts to render clearly what I took to be the most natural (but not always the most obvious) sense.

Restat tantum ut rei publicae Americanae ducentesimum iam annum agenti gratulemur totidemque annos ei precemur.

David Kovacs
Dabam Charlottapoli mense Decembri anno p.C.n. 1988

It remains only to congratulate the Republic on its two hundred years and to wish it two hundred more.

David Kovacs
Charlottesville, December 1988

Marcus Tullius Cicero

Part I

by Harry L. Stern

Marcus Tullius Cicero (106 to 43 BCE) received early literary training largely by writing verse and translating from Greek authors. He began the study of law at sixteen under a succession of the foremost jurists of the day. He also studied oratory from the great leaders at the bar by diligently attending the courts and legislative assemblies. Owing to the preservation of most of his voluminous writings, his life is better known than that of any other ancient personality with the possible exception of St. Augustine. Cicero became the undisputed master of Latin prose style and the creator of Latin philosophical language.

His chief title to fame is that of a man of letters. He was not only the most versatile of all the Latin writers and the greatest master of style, but also one of the most voluminous that have survived. His complete writings comprise more than five thousand printed pages, classified as orations, rhetorical works, philosophical works, letters, and poems. Fifty-seven of his orations have been preserved entirely. Cicero was also a prolific letter writer. Nearly eight hundred have survived as well as about one hundred from correspondents addressed to him.

Cicero produced fifteen philosophical works in the years 46-44 BCE. The most important were the *De Republica*, *De Legibus*, *De Officiis*, *De Amicitia*, and *De Senecute*. These dealt with political philosophy, constitutional theory, morality, friendship, and old age. They were compilations of ancient Greek philosophy as interpreted by Cicero's teachers in the Stoic, Agnostic, and various schools of his own era.

Plato, Aristotle, and other original thinkers who had flourished in the golden age of Athenian ascendency were as distant to Cicero in time as Descartes and Locke are to us today. It was Cicero who developed the Latin language from a provincial dialect to an international language clearly expressing abstract and complicated thought.

In Cicero's era, a truly educated man had to be fluent in the Greek language. Greek had become the dominant language of culture throughout the Near East and the Mediterranean during the three and a half centuries after the death of Alexander the Great. Similarly, in the nineteenth century, men of culture had to be fluent in the French language. Authors from Russia, Poland, the German states, the Austrian Empire, and Greece frequently wrote in French to gain a wider audience for their works.

It was immediately after his death that the Roman Republic of several centuries had collapsed, and the four centuries of the Roman Empire began. The Empire expanded geographically and grew more autocratic until its demise in the fifth century, but the language it took to the remote corners of the known Western World was the Latin of Cicero. Correspondence from Roman Britain, Germany, Spain, North Africa, Egypt, Syria, and the Danube was all sent to Rome in Ciceronian style. When the split with the eastern Empire occurred in the fourth century, inaugurating what became the thousand-year-long Byzantine Empire, Justinian promulgated his Greek language legal code with a Latin translation to extend that code's understanding beyond the then contracting Hellenic sphere of influence.

St. Augustine (354-430 AD) has had exceedingly widespread influence on Catholicism even until our own era. The sixteen volumes of his works are a tribute to Ciceronian Latin. St. Augustine's Latin style was paramount among the Church Fathers until the advent of Thomas Aquinas eight hundred years later. As Christian fiefdoms survived in the feudal era following the short-lived empires of the Goths, Huns, and others who had destroyed centralized Roman power, the churchmen who supported the ruling lords of these fiefdoms kept Ciceronian Latin alive as the language of communication with other Christian communities.

The two most influential of all these churchmen were Albertus Magnus of Cologne (1200-1280) and his star Italian pupil, St. Thomas Aquinas (1225-1274). The latter's *Summa Theologica* is the fusion of Aristotelian thought and Catholic dogma. Among the more prominent exponents of Ciceronian Latin in the sixteenth century were Erasmus and Copernicus; in the seventeenth century Descartes, Spinoza, and Grotius.

From the beginning of the Renaissance, when his complete works were recovered and studied extensively, Cicero became the universally recognized master of Latin prose style. The cultivation of Ciceronian Latin in the European school tradition exercised a marked effect on the development of vernacular prose style in general. In the late nineteenth century, Pope Leo XIII gave Ciceronian Latin a basic place in his reform of Papal Chancery style. His own encyclicals and those of his successors exhibit the deliberate use of Ciceronian language.

Part II

by Harry L. Stern

Those Founding Fathers of the United States of America who had college educations were steeped in the writings of Roman authors whom they nearly all read in the original Latin. Especially noteworthy, perhaps, were John Adams, Thomas Jefferson, and James Madison. They began extensive Latin language instruction at the age of ten to twelve. Some attended private academies; others were taught by private tutors. The basic requirement for acceptance at most colleges was a thorough knowledge of classical Latin and the numerous writers of the ancient Roman world. This requirement sometimes extended to classical Greek and its literature.

The background of many of the delegates to the Constitutional Convention of 1787 included expertise in the Latin language. This was particularly true for the five members chosen to function as a *Committee of Style*. Their mandate was to arrange the agreed-upon articles in proper sequence and revise their form for clarity of language. They completed the elegant digest we revere today between September 6th and September 12th, 1787. Five days later, the Constitution of the United States was adopted after a final vote by the thirty-nine delegates and sent to the states for ratification.

The *Committee of Style* membership had been selected for expertise in written expression, rhetorical skill, and excellence of achievement, coupled with geographic balance to help facilitate acceptance of the final document.

Rufus King

Rufus King

Rufus King (1755-1827) was born in southern Maine (then part of Massachusetts). He attended the private Dummer Academy at the age of twelve. After graduating from Harvard College in 1777, King studied law under Theophilus Parsons, the most eminent legal authority of his era in New England. He served as a Major under Gen. John Sullivan in the key Battle of Rhode Island in August of 1778. That event marked the entry of France as an active ally of the American forces in the Revolutionary War.

Resuming his law studies under Parsons, King passed the bar in 1780. He served numerous terms in the Massachusetts State Assembly and later as a delegate to the Constitutional Convention of 1787 in Philadelphia. King was a persuasive orator who rose to prominence along with Madison, Morris, and Hamilton. He played a major role in creating the final document that became the Constitution of the United States, and then succeeded in gaining its ratification in Massachusetts. He soon left his law practice, moved to New York City and remained there in politics.

Rufus King served several terms as a Federalist in the United States Senate, was a Vice-Presidential and Presidential candidate, and twice was Ambassador to England. However, his greatest accomplishment perhaps was his early and vehement opposition to slavery.

William Samuel Johnson

William Samuel Johnson

William Samuel Johnson (1727-1819) of Connecticut was the son of a prominent clergyman who was the first president of King's College (later Columbia College). He graduated from Yale in 1744, earned his M.A. there three years later, and became a prominent lawyer through personal effort without formal training. He was a Connecticut militia officer in the 1760s, served in both the lower and upper houses of the colonial assembly, and ultimately was on the colonial supreme court.

He also became Connecticut's agent in England and received an honorary degree from Oxford. After the Revolutionary War, Johnson served in the Continental Congress of 1785-1787. His participation in the Constitutional Convention was crucial. He authored the Connecticut Compromise whereby competing New Jersey and Virginia plans resulted in the election of House of Representatives members by popular vote and each state receiving two Senators regardless of size. Johnson was chairman of the *Committee of Style*, a position of great authority he had achieved based on his reputation and prestige.

Johnson later served in the United States Senate and ended his public career as President of Columbia College. He outlived nearly all of the Founding Fathers.

Alexander Hamilton

Alexander Hamilton

Alexander Hamilton (1757-1804) was born on the Caribbean island of Nevis. He learned fluent French from his Huguenot mother, who died when he was eleven. Relatives sent him to New York in 1772 for further education. After a year at Francis Barber's nearby private school, Hamilton matriculated at King's College (now Columbia University). He became a celebrated pamphleteer for the patriot cause in the turbulent years preceding the final break with England, and then organized a company of volunteers prior to being commissioned in 1775. His political writing and active-duty service on Long Island, White Plains, Trenton, and Princeton, brought him to the attention of George Washington, whom he long served as secretary and administrative assistant. Ultimately, Hamilton commanded a regiment in Lafayette's Corp with great distinction at the siege of Yorktown.

Hamilton believed in a strong military and executive branch of government. He practiced law in New York, representing urban business and banking interests. He was a founder of the Federalist Party, the New York Post, the Bank of New York, and the United States Coast Guard. He created the nation's financial system as President Washington's Secretary of the Treasury. He was active in ending the international slave trade. But his major contribution of arguments favoring the United States Constitution in the Federalist Papers helped secure its ratification in New York and the other states that followed. Finally, Hamilton's forceful support of Jay's Treaty cleared the Ohio Valley and Great Lakes region for American expansion at the expense of French interests in Canada. His early death probably deprived the United States of a future President.

Gouverneur Morris

Gouverneur Morris

Gouverneur Morris (1751-1816) had a meteoric rise in politics based on brains, ability, and a persuasive personality. Growing up in New York, he learned French as a youth in a familial setting. He studied both Latin and Greek, reading Homer, Xenophon, Cicero, Caesar, and above all Horace, whose stoicism may have helped shape his world view. He graduated from King's College (now Columbia University) at the age of sixteen. He was admitted to the bar at nineteen, and authored the New York Constitution in 1776 (with Jay and Livingston). That document remained essentially unchanged for half a century.

Elected to the Continental Congress of 1778-1780, Morris was involved at the highest level in military, diplomatic, and financial affairs relating to the Revolutionary War. He then moved to Philadelphia, became a political force there, and was elected to the Pennsylvania delegation to the Constitutional Convention of 1787. Following Thomas Jefferson's long ambassadorship in France, Morris served with great success throughout the French Revolution before returning to private affairs in New York. Although William Johnson was chairman of the *Committee of Style*, the primary wordsmith deciding the ultimate language (probably exceeding even Madison's input) was Morris. He was undoubtedly also the author of the *Preamble*.

James Madison

James Madison

James Madison (1751-1836) studied Latin with a private tutor at the age of twelve. He also learned Greek for the New Testament. After graduating from the College of New Jersey (later Princeton University) in 1771, he spent a year absorbing Old Testament Hebrew. Perhaps more significantly, Madison was thoroughly familiar with the political works of Cicero and the legal texts of Justinian and Grotius. He had also read in Latin the literary works of Virgil, Sallust, Ovid, and Terence. He therefore was keenly aware of the successes and failures of previous democratic and republican eras of self-rule.

Madison served in the Continental Congress at the end of the Revolutionary War and again for Virginia in the mid-1780s. He was a prolific polemicist for a stronger union than the Articles of Confederation provided. He was a leading intellectual who was also persuasive in oral argument, and a key partner for the better-known Thomas Jefferson in advancing the interests of Virginia. Madison was eclipsed perhaps only by Gouverneur Morris in editing the final text of the United States Constitution presented to the delegates for their decisive vote. Madison stayed heavily involved in the politics of the 1790s, became President Jefferson's Secretary of State, and his successor as President of the United States.

The Latin School of Chicago class of 1948. Harry L. Stern is seated in the front row at the far left.

Part III

by Harry L. Stern

In the 1940s, students at the Chicago Latin School began their study of the Latin language in the seventh grade. The first two years featured a vigorous curriculum of grammar, vocabulary, and composition. The initial readings were in Caesar's *Gallic Wars*. During the four years of high school, we read Cicero, Virgil, Horace, Catullus, and other authors from the Golden and Silver ages of classical Latin. I continued to study the Latin language throughout my undergraduate years at Yale. Graduate school in Switzerland included Ciceronian Latin composition.

But even this extensive twelve-year-long background in the Latin language did not adequately prepare me for the project I began forty years ago (in 1977) as a dealer in antiquarian books and manuscripts. In 1983 and again in 1991, I was involved in the purchase of an original printed copy of the Constitution of the United States. What struck me in reading and re-reading this precise and revolutionary document was that it sounded like a translation from some Latin prototype from the Roman Republic.

Knowing that most of the delegates to the Constitutional Convention, but particularly the five members of the *Committee of Style*, were learned in the works of Cicero and the legal texts of the Ancient World, perhaps this Constitution could be turned into Ciceronian Latin. I worked at it for years without success.

Subsequent research revealed that the finest modern writer of classical Latin prose was Professor David Kovacs of the University of Virginia.

17

Fortunately, he agreed to make this translation of the United States Constitution. His text was reviewed by Professor Kevin Newman* of the University of Illinois, the other leading authority on Latin prose composition. Their task was completed in 1987.

* Deceased July 26, 2020

Part IV

NOS, POPULUS CIVITATIUM FOEDERATARUM, UT CIVITATIBUS NOSTRIS PERFECTIUS SOCIATIS IUS FUNDEMUS, OTIUM DOMESTICUM CONROBOREMUS, COMMUNI PROVIDEAMUS DEFENSIONI, UTILITATI SALUTIQUE OMNIUM SERVIAMUS, ET BONA LIBERTATIS ET NOBIS IPSIS ET POSTERIS PAREMUS, EDICIMUS, SCISCIMUS, SANCIMUS UT HANC REI PUBLICAE FORMAM HABEANT CIVITATES FOEDERATAE AMERICAE.

We the People of the United States, in Order to form a more perfect Union, establish Justice, insure domestic Tranquility, provide for the common defence, promote the general Welfare, and secure the Blessings of Liberty to ourselves and our Posterity, do ordain and establish this Constitution for the United States of America.

Caput I

Pars i. Quam legum perferendarum in hac re publica potestatem hae litterae dederint, eam omnem Congressus Civitatium Foederatarum habeto, qui Congressus ex duobus Ordinibus constato, Senatorum scilicet et Delegatorum.

Pars ii. Delegatos altero quoque anno populi singularum Civitatium creanto, in quibus creandis ii soli ius suffragii habento qui et in singulis Civitatibus ordinem numero maiorem legumlatorum creare solent.

Ne quem Delegatum creanto nisi viginiti et quinque annos natum, septem annos Foederatarum Civitatium civem, et incolam, dum creatur, eius Civitatis in qua delectus erit.

Article I

Section 1. All legislative Powers herein granted shall be vested in a Congress of the United States, which shall consist of a Senate and House of Representatives.

Section 2. The House of Representatives shall be composed of Members chosen every second Year by the People of the several States, and the Electors in each State shall have the Qualifications requisite for Electors of the most numerous Branch of the State Legislature.

No Person shall be a Representative who shall not have attained to the Age of twenty five Years, and been seven Years a Citizen of the United States, and who shall not, when elected, be an Inhabitant of that State in which he shall be chosen.

Quot Delegatos habeat quantumque vectigalis pendat quaeque Civitas quae hoc foedere iunguntur iungenturve pro multitudine hominum decernunto, in quam multitudinem numeranto omnes liberos homines, inclusis eis qui se in certum temporis spatium servituti dederunt, omissis indigenis qui vectigalium immunes sunt, accedentibus autem ceterorum hominum tribus ex quinque partibus. Intra annum tertium Congressus Foederatarum Civitatium primo convocati enumeranto populum, postea autem intra decimum quemque annum sicut lege statutum erit. Ne plures sunto Delegati quam unus pro singulis milibus tricenis, ita tamen ut quaeque Civitas unum certe Delegatum habeat. Et donec numeretur populus, liceto Novohanoniensibus tres deligere, Massachusettensibus octo, Rhodiensibus et Providentiae Colonis unum, Connecticutensibus quinque, Noveboracensibus sex, Novocaesareanis quattuor, Pennsylvanianis octo, Delawarianis unum, Marylandianis sex, Virginianis decem, Carolinatibus Septentrionalibus et Australibus quinque utrisque et Georgianis tres.

Si cuius in Civitatis legatione locus vacabit, eius Civitatis Magistratus locum illius supplendum curanto.

Delegati Oratorem vel principem suum nec non alios suarum curatores rerum eligunto; et penes eos solos potestas esto magistratus reos ob publice delicta faciendi.

Representatives and direct Taxes shall be apportioned among the several States which may be included within this Union, according to their respective Numbers, which shall be determined by adding to the whole Number of free Persons, including those bound to Service for a Term of Years, and excluding Indians not taxed, three fifths of all other Persons. The actual Enumeration shall be made within three Years after the first Meeting of the Congress of the United States, and within every subsequent Term of ten Years, in such Manner as they shall by Law direct. The Number of Representatives shall not exceed one for every thirty Thousand, but each State shall have at Least one Representative; and until such enumeration shall be made, the State of New Hampshire shall be entitled to chuse three, Massachusetts eight, Rhode-Island and Providence Plantations one, Connecticut five, New-York six, New Jersey four, Pennsylvania eight, Delaware one, Maryland six, Virginia ten, North Carolina five, South Carolina five, and Georgia three.

When vacancies happen in the Representation from any State, the Executive Authority thereof shall issue Writs of Election to fill such Vacancies.

The House of Representatives shall chuse their Speaker and other Officers; and shall have the sole Power of Impeachment.

Pars iii. Civitatium Foederatarum Senatus binos de quaque Civitate Senatores habeto, a Conventu cuiusque Civitatis electos, qui senos annos hoc munere fungentur, singulis utentur suffragiis.

Statim a comitiis primis cum se in unum congregarint, in tres classes quam potest aequissimas se dividunto; quarum primae classis Senatores usque ad finem secundi anni, secundae classis ad finem quarti, tertiae ad finem sexti munere fungantur ita ut altero quoque anno tertia pars deligatur. Si qui locus vacuus erit vel abdicatione alicuius vel ex alia causa dum intermittitur Conventus illius Civitatis, Magistratibus illius Civitatis ad tempus aliquem suffectum nominare liceto donec Conventus rursus conveniens alium sufficiat.

Ne quem Senatorem creanto nisi triginta annos natum, Civitatium Foederatarum novem annos civem, et incolam, dum creatur, eius Civitatis pro qua Senator creatus erit.

Senatui praesideto Civitatium Foederatarum Praeses Vicarius ita ut sententiam ipse ne dicat nisi Senatorum sententiae pares fuerint.

Alios quoque sibi praefectos eligito Senatus, nec non qui pro tempore praesideat dum Praeses Vicarius vel aberit vel Praesidis vice fungetur.

Section 3. The Senate of the United States shall be composed of two Senators from each State, chosen by the Legislature thereof, for six Years; and each Senator shall have one Vote.

Immediately after they shall be assembled in Consequence of the first Election, they shall be divided as equally as may be into three Classes. The Seats of the Senators of the first Class shall be vacated at the Expiration of the second Year, of the second Class at the Expiration of the fourth Year, and of the third Class at the Expiration of the sixth Year, so that one third may be chosen every second Year; and if Vacancies happen by Resignation, or otherwise, during the Recess of the Legislature of any State, the Executive thereof may make temporary Appointments until the next Meeting of the Legislature, which shall then fill such Vacancies.

No Person shall be a Senator who shall not have attained to the Age of thirty Years, and been nine Years a Citizen of the United States, and who shall not, when elected, be an Inhabitant of that State for which he shall be chosen.

The Vice President of the United States shall be President of the Senate, but shall have no Vote, unless they be equally divided.

The Senate shall chuse their other Officers, and also a President pro tempore, in the Absence of the Vice President, or when he shall exercise the Office of President of the United States.

De magistratibus ob publice delicta reis factis solus iudicato Senatus, quas causas iudicaturi iure iurando se obstringunto vel affirmatione saltem sollemni. Sin autem reus erit Praeses Foederatarum Civitatium, iudicio praesideto Iudex Primus. Neu quemquam damnanto nisi duabus partibus Senatorum qui aderunt consentientibus.

In damnatos ne ultra animadvertunto quam ut loco amoveant interdicantque eis ne postilla ullo honore fiducia emolumento publico fruantur, ita tamen ut per leges eos liceat aliis quaestionibus in ius vocare accusare damnare punire si quid contra leges peccarint.

Pars iv. Quo tempore loco modo Senatorum Delegatorumque comitia habeantur cuiusque Civitatis legumlatores decernunto. Sed liceto semper Congressui de his rebus lege decernere vel decreta mutare, hac re tamen excepta quo loco Senatores deligantur.

Semel certe in annum Congressus coito. Et nisi secus decretum erit, mensis Decembris primae hebdomadis dies alter conveniendi dies certus esto.

Pars v. De comitiis Senatorum Delegatorumve utrum rata sint necne deque numerationibus suffragiorum uterque ordo, Senatorum scilicet et Delegatorum, solus de suis iudicandi habeto potestatem, idque decernendi, num cui per leges liceat Senatori vel Delegato fieri. Et utrique Ordini agere liceto, si maior pars Senatorum vel Delegatorum aderit; sin minus, in posterum res differre nec non absentes adesse cogere quibuscumque poenis utrique Ordini visum erit.

The Senate shall have the sole Power to try all Impeachments. When sitting for that Purpose, they shall be on Oath or Affirmation. When the President of the United States is tried, the Chief Justice shall preside: And no Person shall be convicted without the Concurrence of two thirds of the Members present.

Judgment in Cases of Impeachment shall not extend further than to removal from Office, and disqualification to hold and enjoy any Office of honor, Trust or Profit under the United States: but the Party convicted shall nevertheless be liable and subject to Indictment, Trial, Judgment and Punishment, according to Law.

Section 4. The Times, Places and Manner of holding Elections for Senators and Representatives, shall be prescribed in each State by the Legislature thereof; but the Congress may at any time by Law make or alter such Regulations, except as to the Places of chusing Senators.

The Congress shall assemble at least once in every Year, and such Meeting shall be on the first Monday in December, unless they shall by Law appoint a different Day.

Section 5. Each House shall be the Judge of the Elections, Returns and Qualifications of its own Members, and a Majority of each shall constitute a Quorum to do Business; but a smaller Number may adjourn from day to day, and may be authorized to compel the Attendance of absent Members, in such Manner, and under such Penalties as each House may provide.

Quo modo quibusve normis res suae agantur uterque Ordo provideto; liceto et in suos animadvertere si qui turbidi vel seditiosi fuerint duabusque partibus consentientibus loco emovere.

Commentarios diurnos scribendos curato uterque Ordo interdumque vulgato, eis rebus exceptis quas occultare visum erit. Et si quinta pars eorum qui adsunt iusserit, qui pro quaque sententia, quique contra dixerint in commentariis referunto.

Ne liceto, convocato semel Congressu, alterutri Ordini, nisi alteri quoque placebit, res ultra quam in tertium diem differre neve in ullum alium locum se conferre.

Pars vi. Senatoribus Delegatisque stipendium danto lege decretum, quod stipendium ex aerario publico Civitatium Foederatarum pendunto. Dum Congressui aderint vel eo se conferent vel inde redibunt, sancti sunto quominus deprehendantur nisi quis rei publicae maiestatem laeserit vel scelus nefarium faxit vel vim attulerit; neu si quis quid in utrovis Ordine dixerit contradixeritve, alibi ob hoc rei fiant.

Ne quis Senator Delegatusve per annos magistratus sui ullo munere publico Civitatium Foederatarum fungitor quod per hoc tempus repertum sit vel cuius stipendium per hoc tempus auctum sit; neu si quis munere publico Civitatium Foederatarum fungetur is Senator vel Delegatus esto quamdiu hoc munere fungetur.

Each House may determine the Rules of its Proceedings, punish its Members for disorderly Behavior, and, with the Concurrence of two thirds, expel a Member.

Each House shall keep a Journal of its Proceedings, and from time to time publish the same, excepting such Parts as may in their Judgment require Secrecy; and the Yeas and Nays of the Members of either House on any question shall, at the Desire of one fifth of those Present, be entered on the Journal.

Neither House, during the Session of Congress, shall, without the Consent of the other, adjourn for more than three days, nor to any other Place than that in which the two Houses shall be sitting.

Section 6. The Senators and Representatives shall receive a Compensation for their Services, to be ascertained by Law, and paid out of the Treasury of the United States. They shall in all Cases, except Treason, Felony and Breach of the Peace, be privileged from Arrest during their Attendance at the Session of their respective Houses, and in going to and returning from the same; and for any Speech or Debate in either House, they shall not be questioned in any other Place.

No Senator or Representative shall, during the Time for which he was elected, be appointed to any civil Office under the Authority of the United States, which shall have been created, or the Emoluments whereof shall have been encreased during such time; and no Person holding any Office under the United States, shall be a Member of either House during his Continuance in Office.

Pars vii. Omnes leges quae ad vectigalia exercenda pertinent Delegatorum Ordo prior ferto; sed sicut alias leges liceto Senatui has leges emendare vel emendationibus adsentire.

Si quam legem et Senatus et Delegatorum Ordo pertulerint, priusquam rata fiat, Praesidi Civitatium Foederatarum in manus danto; quam si probarit, nomen suum subscribito; si minus, remittito ad eum Ordinem qui prior rogaverit, eis additis quae contra dicere ei videbitur; qui Ordo, cum quae contra dicta sunt in commentarios fuse rettulerit, denuo rem considerato. Si re denuo considerata duae partes illius ordinis legem pertulerint, ad alterum Ordinem mittunto, additis quae contra dicta sunt, denuo considerandam, cuius Ordinis si duae partes legem pertulerint, rata esto. Sed in huius modi rebus, sententiam quemque Senatorem Delegatumve separatim roganto, et qui legem ferendam censuerint quique non censuerint in commentariis utriusque Ordinis referunto. Si qua lex a Praeside intra decem dies (primo cuiusque hebdomadis die excepto) non remissa erit, ea lex rata esto proinde quasi nomen subscripsisset; at si Congressus absens prohibebit quominus lex remittatur, lex rata ne esto.

Omne iussum, placitum, decretum (iis exceptis quae intermissionem iubent), ad quod quidem confirmandum necesse sit ut et Senatus et Delegatorum Ordo in unum consentiant, ad Praesidem mittunto; neu ratum esto eiusmodi iussum, placitum, decretum nisi ab illo probatum erit vel, si ei displicuerit, denuo pertulerint duae partes utriusque Ordinis, sicut supra de legibus perferendis provisum est.

Section 7. All Bills for raising Revenue shall originate in the House of Representatives; but the Senate may propose or concur with Amendments as on other Bills.

Every Bill which shall have passed the House of Representatives and the Senate, shall, before it become a Law, be presented to the President of the United States; If he approve he shall sign it, but if not he shall return it, with his Objections to that House in which it shall have originated, who shall enter the Objections at large on their Journal, and proceed to reconsider it. If after such Reconsideration two thirds of that House shall agree to pass the Bill, it shall be sent, together with the Objections, to the other House, by which it shall likewise be reconsidered, and if approved by two thirds of that House, it shall become a Law. But in all such Cases the Votes of both Houses shall be determined by yeas and Nays, and the Names of the Persons voting for and against the Bill shall be entered on the Journal of each House respectively. If any Bill shall not be returned by the President within ten Days (Sundays excepted) after it shall have been presented to him, the Same shall be a Law, in like Manner as if he had signed it, unless the Congress by their Adjournment prevent its Return, in which Case it shall not be a Law.

Every Order, Resolution, or Vote to which the Concurrence of the Senate and House of Representatives may be necessary (except on a question of Adjournment) shall be presented to the President of the United States; and before the Same shall take Effect, shall be approved by him, or being disapproved by him, shall be repassed by two thirds of the Senate and House of Representatives, according to the Rules and Limitations prescribed in the Case of a Bill.

Pars viii. Congressui liceto vectigalia, portoria, stipendia, exactiones imponere exercere ut Civitatium Foederatarum aes solvat et communi defensioni et omnium saluti provideat, ita tamen ut in omnibus Civitatibus portoria, stipendia, exactiones paria sint;

item pecuniam fide Civitatium Foederatarum mutuam sumere;

item normas de commercio cum exteris gentibus et inter singulas Civitates et cum Indigenarum tribubus edicere;

item leges aequas de civitate danda promulgare nec non per quas quis se aeri solvendo non esse, salvo capite, profiteatur:

item aurum, argentum, aes ferire; quantumque valeat nummus vel publicus vel exterarum gentium per leges statuere; pondera et modos ad certam formam redigere;

item poenas imponere si qui nummos vel syngraphas Civitatium Foederatarum adulterinas faciunt;

item tabularios mansionesque constituere, viasque in usum tabellariorum publicorum muniendas curare;

item scriptoribus et rerum utilium inventoribus iura propria et peculiaria in scripta inventave sua conservare scientiae et artium fovendarum causa;

item quaestiones adhibere iudiciales, quae Quaestioni Summae adiumento sint;

Section 8. The Congress shall have Power To lay and collect Taxes, Duties, Imposts and Excises, to pay the Debts and provide for the common Defence and general Welfare of the United States; but all Duties, Imposts and Excises shall be uniform throughout the United States;

To borrow Money on the credit of the United States;

To regulate Commerce with foreign Nations, and among the several States, and with the Indian Tribes;

To establish an uniform Rule of Naturalization, and uniform Laws on the subject of Bankruptcies throughout the United States;

To coin Money, regulate the Value thereof, and of foreign Coin, and fix the Standard of Weights and Measures;

To provide for the Punishment of counterfeiting the Securities and current Coin of the United States;

To establish Post Offices and post Roads;

To declare War, grant Letters of Marque and Reprisal, and make Rules concerning Captures on Land and Water;

To raise and support Armies, but no Appropriation of Money to that Use shall be for a longer Term than two Years;

item latrocinia et alia scelera in mari admissa designare et punire nec
non in ea quae contra ius gentium admissa erunt animadvertere;

item bellum indicere, litteras dare quibus magistris navium ius belli
gerendi concedatur, et de praeda terrestri navali ordinare;

item exercitus conscribere et alere, ita tamen ut in plus duorum annorum
spatium ne qua pecunia eis erogetur;

item naves ornare, classiarios alere;

item de copiis terrestribus navalibusque gubernandis ordinandis
praescribere;

item pubem arcessendam curare, ut leges ii exsequantur, seditiosos
comprimant, incursantes propulsent;

item ordinare, armare, disciplina coercere puberes, eamque partem
eorum regere quae Civitatibus Foederatis auxilietur, ita tamen ut
singulae Civitates tribunos eligant, militesque exerceant secundum eas
normas quas statuerit Congressus;

To promote the Progress of Science and useful Arts, by securing for limited Times to Authors and Inventors the exclusive Right to their respective Writings and Discoveries;

To constitute Tribunals inferior to the supreme Court;

To define and punish Piracies and Felonies committed on the high Seas, and Offences against the Law of Nations;

To provide and maintain a Navy;

To make Rules for the Government and Regulation of the land and naval Forces;

To provide for calling forth the Militia to execute the Laws of the Union, suppress Insurrections and repel Invasions;

To provide for organizing, arming, and disciplining, the Militia, and for governing such Part of them as may be employed in the Service of the United States, reserving to the States respectively, the Appointment of the Officers, and the Authority of training the Militia according to the discipline prescribed by Congress;

item ius solum habere in omnibus rebus leges perferre de ea regione quae, singulis Civitatibus concedentibus et Congressu recipiente, sedes rei publicae constituetur (quae regio ne plus decem milia longum latum esto) deque omnibus locis quae, concedentibus iis Civitatibus in quibus sita sunt, empta erunt castrorum in usum vel horreorum vel armamentariorum vel navalium vel quamlibet aliam ob rem;

denique, si quae aliae leges necessariae erunt ad haec munera obeunda, has leges necessarias perferre, nec non ad omnia alia exsequenda quae licebit Civitatibus Foederatis vel magistratuum collegiis publicis vel imperium obtinentibus agere.

Pars ix. Ante annum p. C. n. MDCCCVIII ne interdicito Congressus quominus capita in hanc rem p. immigrent invehanturve si qua cuilibet earum quae nunc sunt Civitatium admittere videatur, ita tamen ut Congressui liceat his capitibus invectis certum vectigal imponere, quod vectigal ne plus decem thaleri pro singulis capitibus esto.

Ne cui deneganto potestatem earum litterarum dandarum quae 'habeas corpus' nuncupantur (quibus litteris imperatur ut corpus accusati adhibeas et qua lege quove iure in custodia teneatur declares) nisi si propter seditionem vel hostium irruptionem saluti publicae necessarium erit.

In singulos homines leges privilegiave ne ferunto, neve ullam legem quae id quod ante legem latam factum est puniat.

To exercise exclusive Legislation in all Cases whatsoever, over such District (not exceeding ten Miles square) as may, by Cession of particular States, and the Acceptance of Congress, become the Seat of the Government of the United States, and to exercise like Authority over all Places purchased by the Consent of the Legislature of the State in which the Same shall be, for the Erection of Forts, Magazines, Arsenals, dock-Yards, and other needful Buildings;—And

To make all Laws which shall be necessary and proper for carrying into Execution the foregoing Powers, and all other Powers vested by this Constitution in the Government of the United States, or in any Department or Officer thereof.

Section 9. The Migration or Importation of such Persons as any of the States now existing shall think proper to admit, shall not be prohibited by the Congress prior to the Year one thousand eight hundred and eight, but a Tax or duty may be imposed on such Importation, not exceeding ten dollars for each Person.

The Privilege of the Writ of Habeas Corpus shall not be suspended, unless when in Cases of Rebellion or Invasion the public Safety may require it.

No Bill of Attainder or ex post facto Law shall be passed.

Ne imponunto in singula capita tributum neve aliud sive in capita sive in agros vectigal nisi ratione habita census vel enumerationis supra statutae.

Ne quod vectigal portoriumve in ullas merces imponunto quae ex ulla Civitate exportantur. Neu, dum commercium cum exteris nationibus regitur vectigalve exigitur, portubus cuiuspiam Civitatis favento magis quam portubus aliarum Civitatium, neu naves in ullam Civitatem vel ex ulla Civitate navigantes oporteat ad ullam aliam Civitatem applicare neve inde solvere neve in ulla portoria pendere.

Ne quam pecuniam ex aerario promunto nisi in aliquem usum lege dicatur; pecuniarumque in aerarium relatarum et ex aerario promptarum rationem recte et palam interdum reddunto.

Ne qua danto Civitates Foederatae insignia ornamentave nobilitatis; neu, si quis munere vel honore in hac re publica fungitur, is ab ullo rege, principe, vel civitate extera ullum donum, emolumentum, munus, insigne cuiusvis generis invito Congressu accipito.

No Capitation, or other direct, Tax shall be laid, unless in Proportion to the Census or enumeration herein before directed to be taken.

No Tax or Duty shall be laid on Articles exported from any State.
No Preference shall be given by any Regulation of Commerce or Revenue to the Ports of one State over those of another: nor shall Vessels bound to, or from, one State, be obliged to enter, clear, or pay Duties in another.

No Money shall be drawn from the Treasury, but in Consequence of Appropriations made by Law; and a regular Statement and Account of the Receipts and Expenditures of all public Money shall be published from time to time.

No Title of Nobility shall be granted by the United States: And no Person holding any Office of Profit or Trust under them, shall, without the Consent of the Congress, accept of any present, Emolument, Office, or Title, of any kind whatever, from any King, Prince, or foreign State.

Pars x. Ne feriunto singulae Civitates foedus ullum, neve in ullam societatem ullumve concilium ineunto; neu litteras danto quibus magistris navium ius belli gerendi concedatur, neu nummum feriunto; neu syngraphas edunto quae nummi instar sint; neu faciunto ut quicquam aliud quam nummus aureus argenteusque in aes solvendum valeat; neu leges privilegiave in singulos homines perferunto neve ullam legem quae id quod ante legem perlatam factum est puniat, neve ullam legem quae efficiat ne quem quae pactus sit praestare oporteat; neve ulla insignia vel ornamenta nobilitatis danto.

Ne imponunto singulae Civitates, invito Congressu, ullum vectigal portoriumve in ea quae importantur exportanturve nisi quae prorsus necessaria erunt ad eas leges exercendas quae res importatas inspici iubent; et cum de summa hulus vectigalis omnes detrahentur impensae, eius quod restat fructum habeto Civitatium Foederatarum Aerarium; Congressuique liceto omnes quae in hisce rebus latae erunt leges emendare eisque moderari. Ne imponunto singulae Civitates, invito Congressu, ullum vectigal in naves mercatorias (prout quaeque earum capax mercium est), neu pace exercitum classemve habento, neu pactum ullum foedusve cum ulla alia Civitate ineunto neu cum ulla civitate extera, neu bellum gerunto nisi ab hostibus in agros suos bellum illatum erit vel in eo versabuntur periculo ut statim agendum sit.

Section 10.   No State shall enter into any Treaty, Alliance, or Confederation; grant Letters of Marque and Reprisal; coin Money; emit Bills of Credit; make any Thing but gold and silver Coin a Tender in Payment of Debts; pass any Bill of Attainder, ex post facto Law, or Law impairing the Obligation of Contracts, or grant any Title of Nobility.

No State shall, without the Consent of the Congress, lay any Imposts or Duties on Imports or Exports, except what may be absolutely necessary for executing it's inspection Laws: and the net Produce of all Duties and Imposts, laid by any State on Imports or Exports, shall be for the Use of the Treasury of the United States; and all such Laws shall be subject to the Revision and Controul of the Congress. No State shall, without the Consent of Congress, lay any Duty of Tonnage, keep Troops, or Ships of War in time of Peace, enter into any Agreement or Compact with another State, or with a foreign Power, or engage in War, unless actually invaded, or in such imminent Danger as will not admit of delay.

Caput II

Pars i. Leges exsequendas curato Civitatium Foederatarum Praeses, qui quattuor annos cum Praeside Vicario, in eiusdem temporis spatium creato, munere fruatur. Quos ambos hunc in modum creanto.

Quaeque Civitas, quo modo quave ratione conventus cuiusque iusserit, tot electores nominato quot Senatores et Delegatos in Congressu habere cuique licebit, ita tamen ut nullus Senator Delegatusve quive ullo honore munere emolumento in re publica fruitur elector fiat.

Article II

Section 1.   The executive Power shall be vested in a President of the United States of America. He shall hold his Office during the Term of four Years, and, together with the Vice President, chosen for the same Term, be elected, as follows.

Each State shall appoint, in such Manner as the Legislature thereof may direct, a Number of Electors, equal to the whole Number of Senators and Representatives to which the State may be entitled in the Congress: but no Senator or Representative, or Person holding an Office of Trust or Profit under the United States, shall be appointed an Elector.

Electores in singulis Civitatibus convenientes binis hominibus tabellis suffragantor, quorum alter saltem ne eandem Civitatem incolito quam ipsi. Et indicem conscribunto omnium hominum quibus suffragati erunt, quot cuique suffragati sint. Quem indicem, cum recognorint et nomina subscripserint, ad sedem rei publicae praesidi Senatus inscriptum mittunto. Qui cum coram Senatorum Ordine et Delegatorum omnes indices resignarit, numeranto suffragia. Praeses is esto qui plurima suffragia tulerit, dummodo maior pars omnium electorum ei suffragati sint; sin autem plures tales erunt et suffragiorum parem numerum habebunt, statim Ordo Delegatorum alterum de iis Praesidem tabellis deligito; et si maior pars suffragiorum nemini contigerit, eodem modo Praesidem deligito Ordo Delegatorum ex iis quinque qui plurima suffragia tulerint. Sed in Praeside deligendo Delegati suffragia per Civitates ita ferunto ut unius Civitatis Delegati uno tantum suffragio utantur. Qua de re agere ne liceto nisi Delegatus vel Delegati ex tribus partibus Civitatium aderunt, neu quisquam Praeses esto nisi a maiore parte Civitatum delectus erit. Sive electores seu Senatores seu Delegati suffragantur, is qui post Praesidem electum plurima suffragia ex electoribus tulerit Praeses vicarius esto. Sed si duo vel plures restabunt qui paria suffragia tulerint, ex eis Praesidem Vicarium tabellis deligito Senatus.

Congressui liceto statuere quo tempore electores deligantur et quo die suffragia ferant, qui dies per Civitates Foederatas idem esto.

The Electors shall meet in their respective States, and vote by Ballot for two Persons, of whom one at least shall not be an Inhabitant of the same State with themselves. And they shall make a List of all the Persons voted for, and of the Number of Votes for each; which List they shall sign and certify, and transmit sealed to the Seat of the Government of the United States, directed to the President of the Senate. The President of the Senate shall, in the Presence of the Senate and House of Representatives, open all the Certificates, and the Votes shall then be counted. The Person having the greatest Number of Votes shall be the President, if such Number be a Majority of the whole Number of Electors appointed; and if there be more than one who have such Majority, and have an equal Number of Votes, then the House of Representatives shall immediately chuse by Ballot one of them for President; and if no Person have a Majority, then from the five highest on the List the said House shall in like Manner chuse the President. But in chusing the President, the Votes shall be taken by States, the Representation from each State having one Vote; A quorum for this Purpose shall consist of a Member or Members from two thirds of the States, and a Majority of all the States shall be necessary to a Choice. In every Case, after the Choice of the President, the Person having the greatest Number of Votes of the Electors shall be the Vice President. But if there should remain two or more who have equal Votes, the Senate shall chuse from them by Ballot the Vice President.

The Congress may determine the Time of chusing the Electors, and the Day on which they shall give their Votes; which Day shall be the same throughout the United States.

Ne cui liceto Praesidi fieri nisi civi in Civitatibus Foederatis nato quive civis iam tum fuerit cum hanc rei publicae formam Civitates asciscent; nec nisi qui quinque et triginta annos natus sit et Civitatium Foederatarum quattuordecim annos incola.

Si quando loco emotus erit Praeses vel obierit vel se abdicaverit vel potestatibus et officiis huius muneris fungi non potuerit, Praesidi Vicario hoc munus deferunto; Congressuique liceto lege constituere, si et Praeses et Vicarius emoti erunt vel obierint vel abdicaverint vel munere fungi non poterint, quinam magistratus Praesidis vice fungatur qui magistratus Praesidis vice fungitor donec aut Praeses rursus officia obire possit vel novus Praeses deligatur.

Stipendium certis temporibus Praesidi danto, quod stipendium intra annos magistratus eius ne augento neu diminuunto; neve intra hoc tempus ullum emolumentum aliud neque de Civitatibus Foederatis accipito neque de ulla earum.

Priusquam magistratum ineat, iure iurando vel affirmatione sollemni in hunc modum se obstringito: "Sancte adiuro (vel affirmo) me ex bona fide omnia Praesidis Civitatium Foederatarum officia exsecuturum, remque publicam Civitatium Foederatarum pro viribus conservaturum tuiturum defensurum."

No Person except a natural born Citizen, or a Citizen of the United States, at the time of the Adoption of this Constitution, shall be eligible to the Office of President; neither shall any Person be eligible to that Office who shall not have attained to the Age of thirty five Years, and been fourteen Years a Resident within the United States.

In Case of the Removal of the President from Office, or of his Death, Resignation, or Inability to discharge the Powers and Duties of the said Office, the Same shall devolve on the Vice President, and the Congress may by Law provide for the Case of Removal, Death, Resignation or Inability, both of the President and Vice President, declaring what Officer shall then act as President, and such Officer shall act accordingly, until the Disability be removed, or a President shall be elected.

The President shall, at stated Times, receive for his Services, a Compensation, which shall neither be encreased nor diminished during the Period for which he shall have been elected, and he shall not receive within that Period any other Emolument from the United States, or any of them.

Before he enter on the Execution of his Office, he shall take the following Oath or Affirmation:—"I do solemnly swear (or affirm) that I will faithfully execute the Office of President of the United States, and will to the best of my Ability, preserve, protect and defend the Constitution of the United States."

Pars ii. Exercitibus et classibus Civitatium Foederatarum imperato Praeses nec non vexillariis singularum Civitatium si quando sub Civitatibus Foederatis stipendium merebuntur; eique liceto a provincias singulas obtinentibus sententiam scriptam postulare de iis rebus quae ad provincias suas pertinebunt: itemque liceto poenam differre vel veniam dare si quis Civitatium Foederatarum leges violarit, iis tantum exceptis qui apud Senatum rei fuerint.

Liceto ei, admonente et consentiente Senatu, foedera ferire dummodo duae partes Senatorum qui adsunt consentiant; et deligito et, admonente et consentiente Senatu, designato legatos et alios oratores ad exteras gentes mittendos, et qui iura civium apud exteras gentes tueantur, iudices qui in Quaestione Summa sedeant, omnesque alios magistratus qui lege instituentur, iis exceptis de quibus creandis in hac constitutione secus provisum est. Sed Congressui liceto minorum magistratuum, si quos ei visum erit, designandorum potestatem vel Praesidi deferre vel iudicibus, vel iis qui provinciis singulis praesunt.

Si qui loci intermittente Senatu vacui erunt, liceto Praesidi suffectos designare, quibus mandetur ut usque eo tantum munere fungantur dum Senatus rursus conveniens rursus intermiserit.

Section 2. The President shall be Commander in Chief of the Army and Navy of the United States, and of the Militia of the several States, when called into the actual Service of the United States; he may require the Opinion, in writing, of the principal Officer in each of the executive Departments, upon any Subject relating to the Duties of their respective Offices, and he shall have Power to grant Reprieves and Pardons for Offences against the United States, except in Cases of Impeachment.

He shall have Power, by and with the Advice and Consent of the Senate, to make Treaties, provided two thirds of the Senators present concur; and he shall nominate, and by and with the Advice and Consent of the Senate, shall appoint Ambassadors, other public Ministers and Consuls, Judges of the supreme Court, and all other Officers of the United States, whose Appointments are not herein otherwise provided for, and which shall be established by Law: but the Congress may by Law vest the Appointment of such inferior Officers, as they think proper, in the President alone, in the Courts of Law, or in the Heads of Departments.

The President shall have Power to fill up all Vacancies that may happen during the Recess of the Senate, by granting Commissions which shall expire at the End of their next Session.

Pars iii. Certiorem interdum Congressum facito Praeses quo in loco res publica sit, eisque deliberantibus ea quae necessaria et utilia iudicarit suadeto; liceto ei, cum res in aliquod discrimen provenerint, vel utrumque Ordinem convocare vel alterum eorum, et si qua inter eos dissensio erit, quonam tempore rursus conveniant, convocare ei liceto in quem diem ei visum erit; legatos aliosque oratores publicos excipito; leges cum bona fide exsequendas curato; omnibusque Civitatium Foederatarum praefectis mandata dato.

Pars iv. Praesidem, Praesidem Vicarium, et omnes alios Civitatium Foederatarum magistratus civiles loco emovento si qui proditionis accusati vel ambitus vel aliorum gravioris notae scelerum maleque commissorum apud Senatum damnati erunt.

Section 3. He shall from time to time give to the Congress Information of the State of the Union, and recommend to their Consideration such Measures as he shall judge necessary and expedient; he may, on extraordinary Occasions, convene both Houses, or either of them, and in Case of Disagreement between them, with Respect to the Time of Adjournment, he may adjourn them to such Time as he shall think proper; he shall receive Ambassadors and other public Ministers; he shall take Care that the Laws be faithfully executed, and shall Commission all the Officers of the United States.

Section 4. The President, Vice President and all civil Officers of the United States, shall be removed from Office on Impeachment for, and Conviction of, Treason, Bribery, or other high Crimes and Misdemeanors.

Caput III

Pars i. Potestatem iudicialem una Quaestio Summa habeto una cum iis minoribus quaestionibus quae Congressus ut res postulat constituet. Iudices qui in his quaestionibus cum Summa tum minoribus sedebunt munere eo usque funguntor quoad se probos et honestos praebebunt, iisque stipendium certis temporibus danto, quod stipendium dum in magistratu manebunt ne diminuunto.

Pars ii. Omnia hi iudicanto quae ad eas res pertinebunt, sive de iusto lege definito agitur sive de aequo, quae aut hac Constitutione movebuntur aut Civitatium Foederatarum legibus aut foederibus a Civitatibus Foederatis factis faciendisve; itemque omnia in quibus de legatis vel oratoribus agetur vel de iis qui iura civium apud exteras gentes tuentur, vel de navibus vel de mercibus nave vectis; itemque omnes lites in quas Civitates Foederatae vocabuntur, omnesque lites quae inter duas vel plures Civitates exsistent, vel inter Civitatem et alterius Civitatis civem, vel inter cives diversarum Civitatium, vel inter cives eiusdem Civitatis qui diversis Civitatibus concedentibus easdem terras sibi adserent, vel inter Civitatem eiusve cives et exteras gentes civesve.

Si qua lis exsistet in qua de legatis vel oratoribus agitur vel de iis qui iura civium apud exteras gentes tuentur vel in qua Civitas quaepiam pars est, in huiusce modi causis primum ad Quaestionem Summam rem deferunto, in ceteris causis supra dictis, non nisi si appellatio fiet, quibus in causis liceto Quaestioni Summae et de legibus et de re iudicare, iis tantum causis exceptis quae Congressus excipiet, secundum normas et leges quae de hisce rebus Congressus perferet.

Article III

Section 1. The judicial Power of the United States, shall be vested in one supreme Court, and in such inferior Courts as the Congress may from time to time ordain and establish. The Judges, both of the supreme and inferior Courts, shall hold their Offices during good Behaviour, and shall, at stated Times, receive for their Services, a Compensation, which shall not be diminished during their Continuance in Office.

Section 2. The judicial Power shall extend to all Cases, in Law and Equity, arising under this Constitution, the Laws of the United States, and Treaties made, or which shall be made, under their Authority;—to all Cases affecting Ambassadors, other public Ministers and Consuls;—to all Cases of admiralty and maritime Jurisdiction;—to Controversies to which the United States shall be a Party;—to Controversies between two or more States;— between a State and Citizens of another State,—between Citizens of different States,—between Citizens of the same State claiming Lands under Grants of different States, and between a State, or the Citizens thereof, and foreign States, Citizens or Subjects.

In all Cases affecting Ambassadors, other public Ministers and Consuls, and those in which a State shall be Party, the supreme Court shall have original Jurisdiction. In all the other Cases before mentioned, the supreme Court shall have appellate Jurisdiction, both as to Law and Fact, with such Exceptions, and under such Regulations as the Congress shall make.

Si qui facinoris rei erunt, eos concilium civium in hanc rem selectorum iudicato, iis exceptis qui apud Senatum accusantur. Causam cognoscunto in ea Civitate in qua facinus admissum erit, sin autem in nulla Civitate admissum erit, in eo loco eisve locis cognoscunto ubi Conventus lege cognosci iusserit.

Pars iii. Ii soli laesae maiestatis rei sunto qui bellum Civitatibus Foederatis intulerint vel hostibus earum se sociarint vel eos adiuverint. Ne quem laesae maiestatis damnanto nisi duo testes de eadem re aperte gesta testimonium dederint vel coram iudicibus confessus erit reus.

Congressui liceto poenam laesae maiestatis statuere, ita tamen ut in stirpem damnatorum ne quid animadvertatur neu quicquam post mortem damnati amittant posteri eius.

The Trial of all Crimes, except in Cases of Impeachment, shall be by Jury; and such Trial shall be held in the State where the said Crimes shall have been committed; but when not committed within any State, the Trial shall be at such Place or Places as the Congress may by Law have directed.

Section 3.   Treason against the United States, shall consist only in levying War against them, or in adhering to their Enemies, giving them Aid and Comfort. No Person shall be convicted of Treason unless on the Testimony of two Witnesses to the same overt Act, or on Confession in open Court.

The Congress shall have Power to declare the Punishment of Treason, but no Attainder of Treason shall work Corruption of Blood, or Forfeiture except during the Life of the Person attainted.

Caput IV

Pars i. Si quid quaevis Civitas de civibus suis lege iusserit vel in tabellas publicas rettulerit vel iudiciis constituerit, id ceterae quoque Civitates ratum habento neu improbanto. Et liceto Congressui legibus generalibus iubere quod testimonium de his legibus tabellis iudiciis sit adhibendum et quid ponderis habeat.

Pars ii. Cives cuiusvis Civitatis omnia ceterarum quoque Civitatium beneficia et immunitates iure habento.

Si quis in quavis Civitate laesae maiestatis aliorumve facinorum accusatus poenam fugerit et in alia Civitate deprensus erit, gubernatore eius Civitatis unde fugerit postulante, tradunto eum abducendum ad eam Civitatem cui licet in id scelus inquirere.

Ne quem eorum qui secundum leges cuiusvis Civitatis servitio vel labori addicti sunt, si in aliam Civitatem fugerit, propter legem ullam eius Civltatis servitute vel labore liberanto sed tradunto, repetente eo cui addictus erit.

Pars iii. Liceto Congressui novas Civitates in hanc sociotatem admittere, ita tamen ut Civitas nova in finibus alterius Civitatis ne efficiatur; neve ex duabus vel pluribus Civitatibus vel ex partibus earum nisi Conventibus earum Civitatium nec non et Congressui placuerit.

Article IV

Section 1. Full Faith and Credit shall be given in each State to the public Acts, Records, and judicial Proceedings of every other State. And the Congress may by general Laws prescribe the Manner in which such Acts, Records and Proceedings shall be proved, and the Effect thereof.

Section 2. The Citizens of each State shall be entitled to all Privileges and Immunities of Citizens in the several States.

A Person charged in any State with Treason, Felony, or other Crime, who shall flee from Justice, and be found in another State, shall on Demand of the executive Authority of the State from which he fled, be delivered up, to be removed to the State having Jurisdiction of the Crime.

No Person held to Service or Labour in one State, under the Laws thereof, escaping into another, shall, in Consequence of any Law or Regulation therein, be discharged from such Service or Labour, but shall be delivered up on Claim of the Party to whom such Service or Labour may be due.

Section 3. New States may be admitted by the Congress into this Union; but no new State shall be formed or erected within the Jurisdiction of any other State; nor any State be formed by the Junction of two or more States, or Parts of States, without the Consent of the Legislatures of the States concerned as well as of the Congress.

Agrum aliasque res quae communiter possident Civitates Foederatae liceto Congressui vendere vel locare et de eis leges vel normas necessarias constituere, ita tamen ut ne quid in hac Constitutione officere videatur quominus agrum sibi asserant Civitates Foederatae vel quaevis Civitatium singularum.

Pars iv. Praestanto Civitates Foederatae Civitatibus singulis ut libere rei publicae in modum gubernentur; et eas ab hostium incursione tuentor nec non, auxilium rogante Conventu Civitatis cuiuspiam vel (si conveniri non potest) magistratu, a civium seditione.

The Congress shall have Power to dispose of and make all needful Rules and Regulations respecting the Territory or other Property belonging to the United States; and nothing in this Constitution shall be so construed as to Prejudice any Claims of the United States, or of any particular State.

Section 4.   The United States shall guarantee to every State in this Union a Republican Form of Government, and shall protect each of them against Invasion; and on Application of the Legislature, or of the Executive (when the Legislature cannot be convened) against domestic Violence.

Caput V

Congressus, si quid in hac Constitutione emendare videbitur, vel ipse emendationes ferto, si duabus partibus utriusque Ordinis placuerit, vel, si postulant Conventus duarum partium Civitatium singularum, concilium convocato ad emendationes ferendas. Quae emendationes, sive a Congressu sive a concilio latae, dummodo pertulerint in tribus partibus Civitatium singularum vel conventus vel concilia in hanc rem convocata (utrumcumque perferendi modum constituerit Congressus), ratae utique sunto proinde ac si pars huius Constitutionis essent; praecavetur tamen ne quid ante annum p.C.n. MDCCCVIII emendationis in capitis primi partis nonae sententias primam et quartam adhibeatur, neve ulla Civitas pari in Senatu suffragiorum numero invita privetur.

Article V

The Congress, whenever two thirds of both Houses shall deem it necessary, shall propose Amendments to this Constitution, or, on the Application of the Legislatures of two thirds of the several States, shall call a Convention for proposing Amendments, which, in either Case, shall be valid to all Intents and Purposes, as Part of this Constitution, when ratified by the Legislatures of three fourths of the several States, or by Conventions in three fourths thereof, as the one or the other Mode of Ratification may be proposed by the Congress; Provided that no Amendment which may be made prior to the Year One thousand eight hundred and eight shall in any Manner affect the first and fourth Clauses in the Ninth Section of the first Article; and that no State, without its Consent, shall be deprived of its equal Suffrage in the Senate.

Caput VI

Si quid ante hanc rem publicam constitutam aeris alieni contraxerint Civitates Foederatae seu quod foedus percusserint quidve pactae erunt, ea omnia eandem habento vim Civitatibus in hanc rei publicae formam redactis quam tum habebant cum priore foedere coniunctae erant.

Haec Constitutio legesque quae secundum eam perlatae erunt, omniaque foedera quae auctoritate Civitatium Foederatarum icta erunt ius sunto summum; et in omnibus Civitatibus iudices secundum hanc legem iudicanto, omnibus neglectis quae in cuiusvis singularum Civitatium constitutionibus vel legibus in contrarium sensum scripta sunt.

Senatores et Delegati iam commemorati nec non in singulis Civitatibus conventuum participes, iudicesque quique rei administrandae praefecti sunt, tam Civitatium Foederatarum quam singularum Civitatium, omnes se iure iurando vel solemni affirmatione obstringunto se hanc rei publicae formam esse defensuros. Sed ne qua lex esto de iis qui muneribus sub auctoritate Civitatium Foederatarum fungentur, ut certam quandam opinionem de rebus divinis profiteantur.

Article VI

All Debts contracted and Engagements entered into, before the Adoption of this Constitution, shall be as valid against the United States under this Constitution, as under the Confederation.

This Constitution, and the Laws of the United States which shall be made in Pursuance thereof; and all Treaties made, or which shall be made, under the Authority of the United States, shall be the supreme Law of the Land; and the Judges in every State shall be bound thereby, any Thing in the Constitution or Laws of any State to the Contrary notwithstanding.

The Senators and Representatives before mentioned, and the Members of the several State Legislatures, and all executive and judicial Officers, both of the United States and of the several States, shall be bound by Oath or Affirmation, to support this Constitution; but no religious Test shall ever be required as a Qualification to any Office or public Trust under the United States.

Caput VII

Dummodo hanc rei publicae formam ratam fecerint concilia ex novem Civitatibus de re publica constituenda convocata, rata esto inter eas civitates qui eam pertulerint.

Scribebamus in concilio de re publica constituenda convocato, consentientibus Delegatis omnium Civitatium quae intererant, a.d. XV Kalendas Octobres anno post Christum natum millesimo septingentesimo octogesimo septimo, post rem publicam Americanam liberam factam duodecimo. Cuius in rei testimonium nomina infra subscripsimus,

De quibus testatur William Jackson, Scriba

G°. Washington
PRAESES, et ex Virginia Legatus

Delawaria
      Geo: Read
      Gunning Bedford jun
      John Dickinson
      Richard Bassett
      Jaco: Broom
Marylandia
      James McHenry
      Dan of St Thos. Jenifer
      Danl. Carroll
Virginia
      John Blair
      James Madison Jr.

Article VII

The Ratification of the Conventions of nine States, shall be sufficient for the Establishment of this Constitution between the States so ratifying the Same.

done in Convention by the Unanimous Consent of the States present the Seventeenth Day of September in the Year of our Lord one thousand seven hundred and Eighty seven and of the Independence of the United States of America the Twelfth In witness whereof We have hereunto subscribed our Names,

attest William Jackson Secretary

G°. Washington
Presidt and deputy from Virginia

Delaware
       Geo: Read
       Gunning Bedford jun
       John Dickinson
       Richard Bassett
       Jaco: Broom
Maryland
       James McHenry
       Dan of St Thos. Jenifer
       Danl. Carroll
Virginia
       John Blair
       James Madison Jr.

Carolina Sept.

       Wm. Blount

       Richd. Dobbs Spaight

       Hu Williamson

Carolina Aust.

       J. Rutledge

       Charles Cotesworth Pinckney

       Charles Pinckney

       Pierce Butler

Georgia

       William Few

       Abr Baldwin

Nova Hanonia

       John Langdon

       Nicholas Gilman

Massachusetts

       Nathaniel Gorham

       Rufus King

Connecticut

       Wm. Saml. Johnson

       Roger Sherman

Novum Eboracum

       Alexander Hamilton

Nova Caesarea

       Wil: Livingston

       David Brearley

       Wm. Paterson

       Jona: Dayton

North Carolina

       Wm. Blount

       Richd. Dobbs Spaight

       Hu Williamson

South Carolina

       J. Rutledge

       Charles Cotesworth Pinckney

       Charles Pinckney

       Pierce Butler

Georgia

       William Few

       Abr Baldwin

New Hampshire

       John Langdon

       Nicholas Gilman

Massachusetts

       Nathaniel Gorham

       Rufus King

Connecticut

       Wm. Saml. Johnson

       Roger Sherman

New York

       Alexander Hamilton

New Jersey

       Wil: Livingston

       David Brearley

       Wm. Paterson

       Jona: Dayton

Pennsylvania

    B Franklin

    Thomas Mifflin

    Robt. Morris

    Geo. Clymer

    Thos. FitzSimons

    Jared Ingersoll

    James Wilson

    Gouv Morris

Pennsylvania

      B Franklin

      Thomas Mifflin

      Robt. Morris

      Geo. Clymer

      Thos. FitzSimons

      Jared Ingersoll

      James Wilson

      Gouv Morris

Emendatio I

Ne quam legem perferto Congressus quae efficiat ut ulla de rebus divinis opinio vel ulla sacrorum forma publice constituatur vel quae sanciat quominus omnes ea sacra quae sibi placeant libere colant; vel quae ius libere loquendi vel scripta per prelum edendi minuat; neu, cum populus ius habeat cum bona pace conveniendi, ulla lex sanciat quominus conveniat populus ut a magistratibus iniuriarum remedium postulent.

Emendatio II

Cum, nisi arma habebit exercita pubes, incolumis stare res publica non possit, ne adimunto ius civile armorum habendorum et ferendorum.

Emendatio III

Ne collocanto pace milites in ullis aedibus invito domino neu bello nisi ut lege provisum erit.

Emendatio IV

Cum id iuris populus habeat ut sancti omnes sint quominus vel ipsi vel domus, res, scripta eorum ab ullo sine iusta causa rapiantur excutianturve, ne violanto hoc ius neve ulli concedunto magistratui ut quemquam excutiant quicquamve rapiant nisi quis iure iurando vel affirmatione sollemni obstrictus causam veri similem adferat subtiliterque describat quem locum scrutari quasque res rapere oporteat.

Amendment I

Congress shall make no law respecting an establishment of religion, or prohibiting the free exercise thereof; or abridging the freedom of speech, or of the press; or the right of the people peaceably to assemble, and to petition the Government for a redress of grievances.

Amendment II

A well regulated Militia, being necessary to the security of a free State, the right of the people to keep and bear Arms, shall not be infringed.

Amendment III

No Soldier shall, in time of peace be quartered in any house, without the consent of the Owner, nor in time of war, but in a manner to be prescribed by law.

Amendment IV

The right of the people to be secure in their persons, houses, papers, and effects, against unreasonable searches and seizures, shall not be violated, and no Warrants shall issue, but upon probable cause, supported by Oath or affirmation, and particularly describing the place to be searched, and the persons or things to be seized.

Emendatio V

Ne quem citanto reum sceleris capitalis vel alioquin flagitiosi nisi a concilio iudiciali maiore accusatur, iis facinoribus exceptis quae, dum in bello praesenti militatur vel in discrimine publico, in militia admissa erunt terrestri vel navali vel inter cuiusvis civitatis vexillarios; neu quemquam eiusdem admissi bis reum faciunto, neu cogunto, dum sceleris reus est, in se testimonium dicere, neu vita, libertate, bonis privanto nisi rite secundum leges cognitum erit; neve in usum publicum bona propria civium sumunto nisi pretio aequo soluto.

Emendatio VI

Si quis cuiuspiam criminis reus est, id iuris habeto ut coram sine mora incorrupte atque integre a concilio iudiciali iudicetur quod eiusdem sit Civitatis in qua facinus admissum sit eiusdemque regionis (quae regiones lege antea constitutae sunto), et ut certior fiat cuius rei accusatus sit et quam ob causam, et ut coram accusantes audiat, et ut habeat quo modo testes adesse cogat qui pro se dicere possint, et ut advocati ope in defensione uti liceat.

Emendatio VII

In omnibus litibus quae secundum commune quod dicunt ius cognoscuntur, in quibus quidem res agantur quae pluris viginti thalerorum aestimantur, ius habento litigantes ut a concilio iudiciali lis iudicetur; et si de quavis re a concilio iudiciali iudicatum erit, ne quis iudex, postmodo appellatus, de eadem re aliter iudicato quam concilio iudiciali fretus secundum commune quod dicunt ius.

Amendment V

No person shall be held to answer for a capital, or otherwise infamous crime, unless on a presentment or indictment of a Grand Jury, except in cases arising in the land or naval forces, or in the Militia, when in actual service in time of War or public danger; nor shall any person be subject for the same offence to be twice put in jeopardy of life or limb; nor shall be compelled in any criminal case to be a witness against himself, nor be deprived of life, liberty, or property, without due process of law; nor shall private property be taken for public use, without just compensation.

Amendment VI

In all criminal prosecutions, the accused shall enjoy the right to a speedy and public trial, by an impartial jury of the State and district wherein the crime shall have been committed, which district shall have been previously ascertained by law, and to be informed of the nature and cause of the accusation; to be confronted with the witnesses against him; to have compulsory process for obtaining witnesses in his favor, and to have the Assistance of Counsel for his defence.

Amendment VII

In Suits at common law, where the value in controversy shall exceed twenty dollars, the right of trial by jury shall be preserved, and no fact tried by a jury, shall be otherwise re-examined in any Court of the United States, than according to the rules of the common law.

Emendatio VIII

Vadimonium ne exigunto nimium neu multas imponunto nimias neu poenas sumunto saevas vel inusitatas.

Emendatio IX

Quod in his litteris quaedam iura enumerantur, non idcirco adimuntur minuunturve cetera iura a populo retenta.

Emendatio X

Quae iura hae litterae nec Civitatibus Foederatis impertiunt nec Civitatibus singulis denegant haec omnia vel Civitatibus singulis servantur vel populo.

Amendment VIII

Excessive bail shall not be required, nor excessive fines imposed, nor cruel and unusual punishments inflicted.

Amendment IX

The enumeration in the Constitution, of certain rights, shall not be construed to deny or disparage others retained by the people.

Amendment X

The powers not delegated to the United States by the Constitution, nor prohibited by it to the States, are reserved to the States respectively, or to the people.

Photo Credits

Page xviii. Cicero. Sculpture by Bertel Thorvaldsen, 1800, in Thorvaldsens Museum, Copenhagen.[1]

Page 6. Rufus King. Painting by Gilbert Stuart, 1820.[1]

Page 8. William Samuel Johnson. Etching by Albert Rosenthal, 1888.[1]

Page 10. Alexander Hamilton. Painting by John Trumbull, 1806.[1]

Page 12. Gouverneur Morris. Painting by Pierre Henri, 1798.[1]

Page 14. James Madison. Painting by John Vanderlyn, 1816.[1]

Page 16. The Latin School of Chicago class of 1948. From the *Sigillum* (Yearbook) of 1948, used by permission of the Latin School of Chicago.

[1]Photo in the public domain, obtained from Wikimedia Commons.

Harry L. Stern III is the son of the originator of the idea to translate the U.S. Constitution into Latin. He lives in Seattle, where he works at the University of Washington's Polar Science Center. He has shepherded the current book into print as a lasting legacy to his father.

Quill Hawk Publishing is an Asian American, woman-owned hybrid publishing company based in Oklahoma dedicated to amplifying diverse voices one story at a time. Amy M. Le is the CEO of Quill Hawk Publishing. Le is a Vietnam War survivor, Congenital Heart Defect (CHD) warrior, and award-winning author of *The Snow Trilogy* and many more books!